THE LITTLE
PUN BOOK

Assembled by ROBERT MARGOLIN

Illustrated by HENRY R. MARTIN

PETER PAUPER PRESS

Mount Vernon, New York

THE
LITTLE
PUN BOOK

I should be punishèd
For every pun I shed:
Do not leave a puny shred
Of my punnish head!

attributed to Samuel Johnson

ONE DAY two old ladies went for a tramp in the woods but he got away.

The explorer came down from the North Pole; when he reached the last Lapp he knew he was at the Finnish line.

The big firecracker said to the little fire-cracker, "My pop's bigger than your pop!"

In the Autumn the farmer buried his father in a corner of the vegetable garden, and next Spring he started hoeing the garden there. "What a way to cultivate his father's memory!" said a neighbor.

A nudist is one who suffers from clothes-trophobia.

Old accountants never die, they just lose their balance.

The man felt like a young colt but he looked like an old 45.

Frozen juices are becoming more popular but most men prefer to squeeze their own tomatoes.

When the principal asked the teacher how long she planned to teach school, she replied, "From here to maternity."

Four fashion models, all wearing Dior gowns, were sitting in a Citroen. When asked what type of car it was, one girl replied, "It's a four Dior job."

Lot's wife didn't turn to salt: she turned to rubber.

The smallest man captured in World War Two was a Japanese who slept on his watch.

Two brothers, who were authors, engaged in a scribbling rivalry.

They hanged a man who had committed murder while drunk. Some one remarked, "This time he took one drop too many!"

One black bird asked another, "Bred any good rooks lately?"

A good masseur leaves no stern untoned.

The three fastest ways of sending news are telephone, telegraph and telewoman.

Mr. Chan was a manufacturer of teakwood stands. For several weeks he noticed that a stand or two was stolen each night. Seeing small footprints near the door of his shop, he thought a small boy was the culprit. To set a trap he dug a large pit and covered it with branches. Next morning he looked in the pit and there was a bear clutching two stands. "Aha," he exclaimed, "Boy-foot bear with teaks of Chan."

An unscrupulous lawyer stayed up with a pretty widow all one night trying to break her will.

A shepherd, when asked why he kept giving aspirin to his sheep, replied, "It's just a question of baa relief."

An ass can never be a horse, but he can be a mayor.

A Model-T Ford is like a schoolroom because it has a lot of little nuts inside with a crank up front.

The electric chair is period furniture. It ends a sentence.

A kibitzer is one with an interferiority complex.

Absinthe makes the heart grow fonder.

Goliath was surprised when David hit him with a stone because such a thing never entered his head before.

Mama broom told papa broom, "We're going to have a little whisk broom." Papa replied, "How is that possible? We haven't even swept together."

A fad is in one era and out the other.

There was a knock at the hospital-room door. "Who goes there," said the patient, "friend or enema?"

The snuff salesman is a man who goes around putting his business in other people's noses.

When the baker's union refused to bake the Girl Scout cookies, one labor wit remarked, "It's a case of girl meets boycott."

A room full of married people is empty because there isn't a single person in it.

A woman, fond of trimming her front lawn with a nail scissors, said, "That's all there is. There isn't any mower."

Two cannonballs got married and had beebies.

A society playboy is a cashanova.

A couple went on a date Dutch treat and danced check to check.

What is the difference between an ambassador and a hot dog? An ambassador wears full dress, a hot dog just pants.

What is the difference between a stoat and a weasel? They are weaselly distinguishable because they are stoatally different.

You can tell girl pancakes from boy pancakes by the way they are stacked.

Written on a menu in a Texas restaurant: "Remember the à la mode!"

Children are like flannel because they shrink from washing.

A burlesque queen got a strip-de-carcass infection.

When a group of miniature cattle were put in the Sputnik, it became the herd shot round the world.

A man moved to Kansas City with the firm belief that Missouri loves company.

Wife: You were more gallant when I was a gal.

Husband: You were more buoyant when I was a boy.

A girl cocker spaniel used to meet the postman down the street and proudly carried the letters home in her mouth, until one day when she got a litter from her boyfriend.

An empty purse is always the same because there is never any change in it.

Once a hunter in the woods lost his dog, so he put an ear to a tree and listened to the bark.

A young Spanish girl was named Carmen Cohen. Her mother called her Carmen and her father called her Cohen. By the time she was twelve, she didn't know if she was Carmen or Cohen.

A Mexican girl said to another, that she had the handsomest husband in Mexico. "No, he isn't," said the other, "you should 'ave seen the Juan that got away."

College bred is a four-year loaf made out of the old man's dough.

The farmer named his rooster Robinson because he Crusoe.

During the depression everyone was eating frankfurters, and one man said, "These frankfurters taste like meat at one end and bread crumbs at the other." Someone retorted, "Yeah! these days it's impossible to make both ends meat."

A cow, under analysis, claimed she had a fodder complex.

Sunbathing is a fry in the ointment.

Popular paperbacks always come from the trite side of the racks.

Christmas is the time of year when bosses throw their dogs a bonus.

A flourishing Jewish community in Boston is known as the Back Bagel District. They're even starting a lox and hounds club.

A prominent Turk got an audience with the Sultan who said, "I don't know your name, but your fez is familiar."

Use "conscience-stricken" in a sentence: Don't conscience-stricken before they're hatched.

Joseph was the straightest man in the Bible and so King Pharaoh made a ruler out of him..

The French horn player whose toupee fell in his instrument spent the whole evening blowing his top.

Magic carpets from Arabia are powered by Turban engines.

The Declaration of Atomic Warfare says that all men are cremated equal.

Charles Poore concluded his review of a French art book with, "I speak more in Seurat than in Ingres."

An anthologist is one who likes to spend a quiet evening at home raiding a good book.

The football coach, when his star half-back was sulking in the restaurant toilet, said, "See what the back in the boys' room will have."

"Speaking of bathing," said the tramp, "I bathed in the spring of '46."

Robinson Crusoe is responsible for the forty-hour week. He had all his work done by Friday.

A college lad was dawdling over breakfast one morning finishing his coffee and reading *Canterbury Tales*. His friend came into the coffee-shop and asked, "What have you got there?" The boy answered, "Nothing except my cup and Chaucer."

A press agent is one who is willing to put your feat in his mouth.

Horses have six legs because they have forelegs in front and two legs behind.

The trouble with Verlaine was that he was always chasing Rimbauds.

A writer once boasted, "I write some of Jimmy Durante's best material." At which a friend sneered, "Nose dropper."

A man is trying to cross-breed hens with a racing form so they can lay odds.

Sign on wooden bowl from which George Washington ate bread soaked in milk, "George Washington slupped here."

When a customer demanded an out-of-print cookbook, the bookstore manager replied, "Madam, we cannot have archaic and eat it too."

When the famous drunkard held open house, his friends all said: "Let's dine on the sotted lion."

A bustle is like a historical romance. Both are fictitious tales based on a stern reality.

A man, observing two small wigs on stands in a wig shop, commented, "They're alike as toupees."

The difference between a book and a bore is: you can shut up a book.

A doctor called fat ladies who worry about their weight "Hippochondriacs."

The Danes refused the visit of the Nautilus to avoid something from Groton in the state of Denmark.

A man was asked if he played any instrument. "At home," he said, "I play second fiddle."

On his way to a restaurant in an Italian community, Abe Lincoln got lost. Unable to find the envelope on which he had written the directions, he said, "Good Lord! I've lost the Spaghettisburg address."

A brilliant but tactless talker often finds himself coruscating on thin ice.

Beautiful Spanish senoritas are a snare Andalusian.

There is a Skid Row saloon where the patrons enter optimistically and leave mistyoptically.

Adam is not the first man mentioned in the Bible, but Chap One.

If you take care of your peonies, the dahlias will take care of themselves.

When a wit keeps hearing his stories told back to him, it's a case of the tale dogging the wag.

A Spanish bus driver yelled at the passengers, "I don't want all you Basques in one exit."

An insect collector, watching an insect with long feelers, and a beetle, remarked, "Ah, Antennae and Coleoptera."

A discharged record spinner: a slipped-disc jockey.

"If you can make a joke on any subject," roared the king to his jester, "try making one on me." "Ah," said the jester, "the king is not a subject."

A gangster at the Valentine-Day Massacre funeral remarked, "They should of put all them yeggs in one casket."

A groom should never see his wife before the wedding because too many looks spoil the troth.

A nuclear physicist is reported to have too many ions in the fire.

Any stigma can be used to beat a dogma.

The big social event of a noted fountain pen company is its Pen Point Ball.

A timid lion tamer kept looking for a protection claws in his contract.

If a biscuit is a soda cracker, an ice pick is a water cracker.

When Groucho Marx was shooting elephants in Africa, he found their tusks hard to remove, and said, "In Alabama the Tuscaloosa."

Great aches from little toe-corns grow.

A baseball pitcher with a sore arm was in the throws of agony.

As for any broken dictaphone: it goes without saying.

A writer on Darryl Zanuck's payroll in Hollywood replied to a rival studio that wanted to hire him, "My heart belongs to Fox, lock, stock and Darryl."

When the Rev. Spooner's hat blew away he cried, "Won't somebody pat my hiccup?" And when he dropped his cat on the floor he would always remark, "See how she pops on her drawers."

A man signed a letter he sent to a garden magazine as Constant Weeder.

A girl once told an eager-fingered piano player to keep his dissonance.

When a man asked his wife if she thought his friend could go to a masquerade as Napoleon, she replied, "Of Corsican."

Kiddies call their tricycles tot rods.

Do you know what happened to the girl who swallowed a spoon? She couldn't stir.

In baseball-mad Chicago, a man tried to teach his wife German. He asked "Was sagst du?" She replied, "They lost 7-1."

Adam and Eve were thrown out of the Garden because they were too noisy — they raised Cain.

An astronomer was asked about flying saucers and replied, "No comet."

A thrice-married philosophy professor put divorce before Descartes.

A clergyman was greeted by a friendly parishioner and remarked, "I can't remember your name but your faith is familiar."

Literary teas are fetes worse than death.

A literary critic after judging a competition for avant garde poetry groaned and said, "I'm suffering from new-writers."

The weakest animal in the world is a frog: he will croak if you touch him.

Eli Whitney caught one of his neighbor's slaves burglaring his bar, went to the next plantation and shouted, "Get your cotton picking hands out of my gin."

As old Noah remarked ungrammatically while the animals were boarding the ark, "Now I herd everything."

Two tramps were going down the street on a hot Easter Sunday, grumbling. "Who are they?" asked one man. "Just a couple of hot cross bums," exclaimed the other.

All egoists have the screaming me-me's.

When Fritzie said she had gotten a pearl out of an oyster, Mitzie replied that *she* had gotten a diamond out of an old crab.

Mr. and Mrs. Wong lived happily in Manila until a sailor came into their lives. Mrs. Wong gave birth to a baby that did not look oriental at all. Mr. Wong took his wife to the local sage, told his story, and asked his judgment. The sage said, "I'm sorry, but two Wongs don't make a white."

A fellow sat on the front steps of the New York Public Library trying to read between the lions.

A hermit was picked up for speeding. The charge: recluse driving.

A clock is like a river because it won't run long without winding.

The moon affects the untied as well as the tide.

A man, while carving a tongue for dinner, allowed it to fall on the floor. "Forgive me," he said to his guests, "for that unfortunate slip of the tongue."

A shepherd came to the edge of a frozen lake, one December day. He knew he could save time by taking the sheep across it. As he was hauling the leader down the bank, a farmer rushed out and said, "See here, you can't pull the wool over my ice."

A Peruvian prince fished a beautiful maiden out of a lake and made her his before the Inca was dry.

A man bought two fishes and had three when he got home because he had two flounders — and one smelt.

A duck, a frog and a skunk went to the circus. Tickets were a dollar. Who got in, and who didn't? — The duck got in because she had a bill. The frog got in on his green-back. But the poor old skunk couldn't get in because he had only a scent, and it was a bad one at that.

After a Tokyo murderer was hanged one winter morning, one GI remarked to another, "There seems to be a little Nip in the air this morning."

A man visiting in France saw Françoise Sagan riding in a sports car and said, "I see they've hitched their Sagan to a car."

Even worse than raining cats and dogs is hailing taxis.

When a man marries he gets sixteen wives: four richer, four poorer, four better, four worse.

Two ghosts drifted into a tavern and asked the bartender, "Do you serve spirits here?"

The man who murders his mother in a garret is a worthy person, because he is above committing a crime.

A man trying for a part in "Guys and Dolls" failed to meet the requirements of Frank Loesser and his wife. He said, "I owe my predicament to the evil of the two Loessers."

The day an Egyptian funeral bark was found outside Cairo, a man called the curator of the Metropolitan Museum and said, "Well, pal, you must be licking your Cheops."

A movie producer, tired of searching for and training new talent, felt that he had too many acts to grind.

A restaurant customer demanded lamb chops au gratin, so the waiter shouted to the kitchen, "Cheese it, the chops."

A lady who had a pair of candlesticks fashioned after two nude figures called them her scandalabra.

The man who thought he was signing up as skipper on the good ship Matrimony when he married the widow, soon discovered that he was only the Second Mate.

Your sense of touch suffers when you are ill because you don't feel well.

At one time most of the girls in Utah married Young.

A man once took milk of amnesia to forget his troubles.

A Greek professor tore his suit and took it to a tailor named Acidopolous. The tailor looked at the suit and said, "Euripides?" "Yes," said the professor, "Eumenides?"

A young boy, on seeing his mother knock out his father with a heavy object, remarked, "She conks to stupor."

DEFINITIONS:

Alaska — A prelude to "No"

Automaton — One who eats in the automat

Buccaneer — Current price of corn

Flattery — An apartment house

Gubernatorial — A peanut in swimming

Incongruous — Where the laws are made

A new book has been published about a goat who ate a rabbit. The review called it "A clear case of a hare in the butter."

A violinist, when asked if it was difficult to string a violin replied, "It takes guts."

A cannibal chief said a certain missionary shouldn't be boiled for dinner because he was a friar.

A new magazine for beginning gardeners is being published with the title of "Trowel and Error."

Two skunks, born gamblers, played cards for a scent a point.

In an argument about various editions of the Bible, a woman murmured, "Chacun à son Gutenberg."

The Beggars Opera, written by John Gay and produced by John Rich, was said to have made Rich gay and Gay rich.

A pig should never get sick because he'll have to be killed before he is cured.

A sea-scout leader offered leftover food to all in tents and porpoises.

An ice sculptor enjoys nothing more than working on a deep frieze.

A man called a dry cleaner who had his pants for a long time and said, "If they aren't back in one hour, I'm suing for promise of breeches."

When a lovely young lady at King Arthur's court crept into the castle at four o'clock one morning, she whispered to the guard, "What a knight!"

A couple of ancient Romans decided to burn down the city. One said, "We might be too late. I hear Nero has the same idea." The second said, "Let's beat him to it and eliminate the fiddle man."

Funny thing about the way a horse eats — he eats best when he hasn't a bit in his mouth.

Three Oxford professors in London were accosted by a bevy of street-walkers. The specialist in Barchester novels called them "a chapter of trollops," the Shakespearean scholar called them "a flourish of strumpets," and the short story writer said, "an anthology of pros."

An American met an Italian in Joe's bar. One round of drinks followed another and finally the Italian passed out. The American boasted, "I'm the first man that ever drank a Venetian blind."

An explorer in darkest Africa was captured by cannibals. Each night they would prick his arm with a spear and drink some of his blood. Finally in desperation he cried, "This is the last time you're going to stick me for drinks."

Sign on an auto repair shop, "May we have the next dents?"

She was a nicely reared girl. And she wasn't half bad from the front either.

Sign in reducing salon, "A word to the wide is sufficient."

Children born in houses of ill fame are brothel's sprouts.

Mrs. Bigger had a baby who was bigger than she was, because he was a little Bigger.

Another name for the Rodgers and Hammerstein musical about Anna and the King of Siam might have been "Babes in Thailand."

A rancher couldn't keep his hands off his beautiful wife and finally had to fire every one of them.

Lady Godiva was the world's greatest gambler because she put everything she had on a horse.

Anyone can have four hands by doubling his fists.

The guy who insists on drinking before driving puts the quart before the hearse.

If gossips would tend more to their knitting, they wouldn't get tangled up in so many yarns.

The left side of an apple pie is the part that isn't eaten.

A baby usually wakes up in the wee-wee hours of the morning.

The Pope received the gift of an electric blanket which was called the Purple Papal Heater.

A wolf is like a modern dry cleaner because he works fast and leaves no ring.

In Saudi Arabia an Arab sheik fell off a carnival merry-go-round and was promptly gobbled up by the second of three hungry sheep. The carnival owner shook the sheep and said, "Middle lamb, you've had a Dizzy Bey."

The sailor who relaxed his dates with wine had port in every girl.

The ink drop was crying because his daddy was in the pen.

The mother potato said to her daughter, "Don't marry Lowell Thomas. He's just a commentator."

The burglar tiptoed into the drugstore because he was afraid he'd wake the sleeping pills.

A man was talking about how he made so much money, the taxes were beginning to irk him. His friend commented, "It's nice irk if you can get it."

Sign over drinking fountain, "Old Faceful."

A man was awarded five thousand dollars after being punched by an angry tailor. Every clout has a silver lining.

The doctor passed a nurse in the corridor. He cauterize and winked. She interne winked back.

In a bridge game at the White House an Eisenhower finesse failed and he went down two tricks. It was the first time anyone had dared to set a precedent.

A beautiful young lady tugged constantly at her dress and wiggled uncomfortably. She was obviously a chafing dish.

A disc jockey lived on spins and needles and finally won an award for his old plaque magic.

The maid who had never been kissed was a lass and a lack.

Indians wore feathers in their hair to keep their wigwam.

A sailor is a wolf in ship's clothing.

When the lion-hunter failed to return to camp, one of his fellow-hunters shook his head and said, "He must have disagreed with something that ate him."

Two scoundrels fleeced the richest citizen in Casablanca. As they made off with the boodle, one remarked, "We must do this Moor often."

A man has the right to scold his coffee when he has more than sufficient grounds.

A baker perfected a new variety of doughnut he called the Phyfe — hoping that all antique lovers would buy his dunkin' Phyfes.

An Irish literary critic was groaning after reading too many new authors. "You'd be happier," said a friend, "if you'd just read Joyce and Synge."

A sailor on a whaling ship fell overboard and was swallowed by a whale. The captain and crew took off after the whale and managed to beat the tar out of him.

A gardener at Buckingham Palace stole a chair belonging to Queen Elizabeth and hid it in his greenhouse. He was speedily apprehended, proving that people who live in glass houses shouldn't stow thrones.

A chicken incubator offered: "Cheepers by the dozen."

Sign on a frankfurter stand: "What foods these morsels be."

The captain of an undermanned sailing ship was offered a consignment of hardened convicts during the Napoleonic Wars. "Nothing doing," he protested. "Too many crooks spoil the sloop."

A swami went to the butcher shop to buy some liver. The butcher, seeking to put one over on the swami, beckoned his clerk, and said, "Weigh down upon the swami's liver."

When the little chicken found an orange in his mother's straw box, the little chicken said, "Look at the orange marmalade."

The smallest body of water in the U.S. is Lake Inferior.

A mink gave up psychoanalysis because it couldn't achieve a transfurance.

The new name for doctor-infested Park Avenue is Malady Lane.

A baker who chopped up his French loaves with a cleaver, decided to save time by chopping several at once, and bought a really big one. "Look what I've found," he said to his helper, "I've found a four-loaf cleaver."

A Greek demolition firm is called Edifice Wrecks.

What was the most unusual meal ever eaten? When Ben Belly came home for dinner, he bolted the door, drank from the bedspring, ate scallops from the curtains and a leak from the faucet, took a few hot dogs he had bread himself, and a roll on the floor, and washed all this down with whine from the cat. Then he swallowed the upper story whole, took a few dates from the calendar, and a plumb from his carpenter's kit. He also had tea from his golf-bag. An hour later he didn't feel so good, and he threw up the window.

A cat is longer at night than in the morning because he is taken in in the morning, and let out at night.

When the cannibal ate the missionary it was a case where one man's meat was another man's parson.

The garbagemen's ball was a swill affair.

When Ravel was madly in love with a girl from the Left Bank who was deaf, he wrote "Deafness and Chloe."

A man called on a judge one evening during the dinner hour. The maid answered the door and said, "I'm sorry but his Honor is at steak."

An Arab lady didn't return to her husband's tent till the grey of dawn one morning. Her excuse was, "I was sitting up with a sheik friend."

A man, on hearing that the famous Dublin poet George Russell (known as A.E.) had just lost his temper, remarked, "You mean A.E.'s Irish rose."

As one female TV star said to another when the latest ratings were published, "Don't look now, dear, but your show is slipping."

An Irishman told his chiropodist, "Me fate is in your hands."

Hurricanes are now named after women because there is no such phenomenon as a himmicane.

Employees of a New York candle factory have it pretty soft. They only work on wick ends.

Two old ladies went to a baseball game with a bottle of Four Roses and by the bottom of the fifth the bags were loaded.

The upper crust of society is composed of a lot of crumbs held together by dough.

One man's Mede is another man's Persian.

Divorce and re-marriage: one man's mate is another man's poison.

A lady who suffered on an ocean crossing sent home the following telegram: "Sic transit."

The bridal day is when a man and a woman go to the halter.

Use "fiddlestick" in a sentence:
If you sleep in a bed that is too short your fiddlestick out.

A press agent is a man who hitches his braggin' to a star.

Man who leans backward wishes to meet woman who leans forward. Object: One Enslanted Evening.

The man who altered his will eleven times in two years was a fresh heir fiend.

Some marriage brokers like to go widow shopping.

A new type of fiction, combination horse opera and mystery, is called a whoadunit.

A bell ringer got tangled up in his rope and tolled himself off.

A farmer had a son who went to New York and became a bootblack. Now the farmer makes hay while the son shines.

Two old stags were chatting in the forest. One said, "Look at that deer making a fool of herself for two bucks." The other sighed, "I could use a little doe myself."

A gossip columnist is one who writes other's wrongs.

The things a man's wife buys at auctions can keep him baroque.

A college president warned the alumni chairman against requesting too much money at one time by saying, "Don't put all your begs in one ask it."

An irate poker player once cried, "I am being trey-duced."

A yes-man said to his employer, "You can't prove nodding by me."

At Prague a bath-house attendant tried to separate the men from the women by saying, "Separate Czechs, please."

An entomologist, when asked how his new book was progressing, replied, "It will be okay as soon as I get the bugs out of it."

The business-like pawnbroker's daughter wouldn't allow much on the couch.

A Japanese girl who had been dating a GI gave birth to a blue-eyed blond baby. "Occidents will happen," she said.

Greta Garbo is rumored to have dreamed one night that she sprinkled grass seed in her hair. She awoke the next morning and exclaimed, "I want to be a lawn."

The girls at a beauty shop went out on strike, and picketed the shop. While on strike one of the girls got smallpox. The boss called at union headquarters and roared, "This time you're going too far. My picket has been pocked."

In commenting about Esther Williams, someone said, "A lot of water has flowed over this dame."

A housewife sent her husband to the store for cheese. He walked into the store and said, "Take me to your liederkranz."

A father spent a fortune sending his son to college and got only a quarter-back.

A movie star pointed to her legs and said, "They're still see worthy."

A gold digger is a human gimmee pig.

A mean little boy on the beach left no tern unstoned.

A Texas woman calls her ranch "Focus" because it is where her sons raise meat.

Two German lads were proceeding gingerly along a narrow mountain ledge with their mother. Below them was a drop of a thousand feet. One of the boys suddenly realized that their mother had disappeared. He called back to his brother, saying, "Look Hans, no Ma!"

A man bumped into an old friend in New Orleans and muttered, "How's bayou?"

Nowadays children of musicians should be boptized.

THAT'S ALL!